Amazing Ears

Contents

All Ears

Ears are for hearing sounds. Most animals have ears, but not all ears look the same.

Do You Know?

Animals need to listen for sounds of danger.

Whose ears are these?

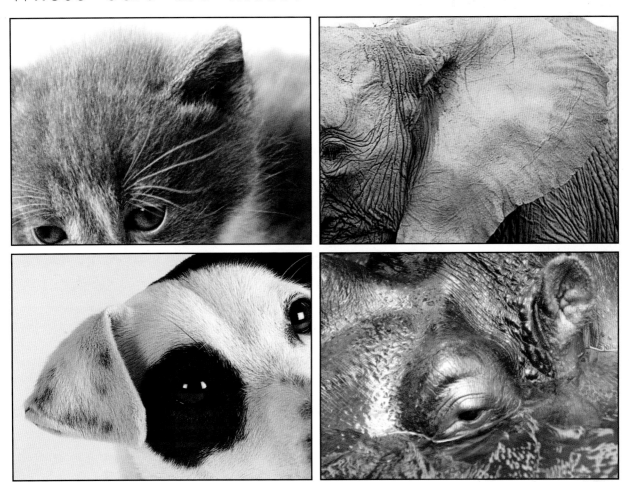

Cat and Dog Ears

Cats and dogs can hear very well. They can hear some sounds that humans can't hear.

Most cats have small, pointed ears.

Do all these dogs' ears look the same?

Rabbit Ears

Rabbits move their ears a lot. This helps them hear sounds from all around.

Do You Know?

Ears can show how an animal is feeling. Rabbits and hares put their ears back when they are angry or scared.

Elephant Ears

Elephants have the biggest ears of all animals.
They can flap their ears to keep cool.

Do You Know?

Mother elephants flap their ears against their bodies to call their babies.

Hippopotamus Ears

A hippo's nose, eyes, and ears are on the top of its head. It can keep most of its body under the water but still listen for danger.

Do You Know?

A hippo can close its ears when it has its head under the water. This keeps the water out.

Look Closely

Some animals have ears that are hard to see. Have you ever seen the ears of a fish or a bird?

A fish hears through tiny holes on its head.

Birds' ears are often covered by tiny feathers.

A lizard has small ear openings on its head.

No Ears

Some creatures have no ears.
But they can still "hear"
when danger is near.

These insects have no ears. They "hear" by feeling vibrations.

Index